STATE OF MICHIGAN.

[Doc. No. 6.]

In Convention to Revise the Constitution, 1850.

Articles of the Constitution, as referred to the Committee on Arrangement and Phraseology.

ARTICLE —.

Bill of Rights.

§ 1. All political power is inherent in the people.

§ 2. Government is instituted for the protection, security and benefit of the people; and they have the right at all times to alter or reform the same, and to abolish one form of government and establish another, whenever the public good requires it.

§ 3. No man or set of men are entitled to exclusive or separate privileges.

§ 4. Every person has a right to worship Almighty God according to the dictates of his own conscience; and no person can of right be compelled to attend, erect, or support, against his will, any place of religious worship, or pay any tithes, taxes, or other rates, for the support of any minister of the gospel, or teacher of religion.

§ 5. No money shall be drawn from the treasury for the benefit of religious societies, or theological or religious seminaries, nor property belonging to the State be appropriated for any such purposes.

§ 6. The civil and political rights, privileges and capacities of no individual shall be diminished or enlarged on account of his opinions or belief concerning matters of religion.

§ 7. Every person may freely speak, write and publish his sentiments on all subjects, being responsible for the abuse of that right; and no law shall be passed to restrain or abridge the liberty of speech or of the press. In all prosecutions for libels, the truth may be given in evidence to the jury; and if it shall appear to the jury that the matter charged as libellous is true, and was published with good motives and for justifiable ends, the party shall be acquitted; and the jury shall have the right to determine the law and the fact.

§ 8. The person, houses, papers and possessions of every individual shall be secure from unreasonable searches and seizures; and no warrant to search any place or to seize any person or things, shall issue without describing them, nor without probable cause, supported by oath or affirmation.

§ 9. The right of trial by jury shall remain inviolate, but shall be deemed to be waived in all civil cases, unless demanded by one of the parties, in such manner as shall be directed by law; and the Legislature may authorize a trial by a jury of a less number than twelve men.

§ 10. In all criminal prosecutions, the accused shall have the right to a speedy and public trial by an impartial jury, which may consist of less than twelve men in all courts not of record; to be informed of the nature of the accusation; to be confronted with the witnesses against him; to have compulsory process for obtaining witnesses in his favor; to have the assistance of counsel for his defence.

§ 11. No person, after acquittal upon the merits, shall be tried for the same offence; all persons shall, before conviction, be bailable by sufficient sureties, except for murder and treason, when the proof is evident or the presumption great; and the privilege of the writ of *habeas corpus* shall not be suspended, unless when, in case of rebellion or invasion, the public safety may require it.

§ 12. Every person has a right to bear arms for the defence of himself and the State.

§ 13. The military shall in all cases and at all times be in strict subordination to the civil power.

§ 14. No soldier shall, in time of peace, be quartered in any house without the consent of the owner or occupant; nor in time of war, but in a manner prescribed by law.

§ 15. Treason against the State shall consist only in levying war against it, or in adhering to its enemies, giving them aid and comfort; no person shall be convicted of treason, unless on the testimony of two witnesses to the same overt act, or on confession in open court.

§ 16. No bill of attainder, ex-post facto law, or law impairing the obligation of contracts, shall be passed.

§ 17. Excessive bail shall not be required; excessive fines shall not be imposed; and cruel or unusual punishments shall not be inflicted, nor shall witnesses be unreasonably detained.

§ 18. The property of no person shall be taken for public use without just compensation therefor. Private roads may be opened in the manner to be prescribed by law; but in every case the necessities of the road and the amount of all damage to be sustained by the opening thereof, shall be first determined by a jury of freeholders; and such amount, together with the expenses of proceedings, shall be paid by the person or persons to be benefitted.

§ 19. The people have the right peaceably to assemble together, to consult for the common good, to instruct their representatives, and to petition the Legislature for a redress of grievances.

§ 20. No person shall be compelled in any criminal case to be a witness against himself, nor be deprived of life, liberty or property, without due process of law.

§ 21. Aliens who are, or who may hereafter become, *bona fide* residents of this State, shall enjoy the same rights in respect to the possession, enjoyment and inheritance of property, as native born citizens.

§ 22. Neither slavery nor involuntary servitude, unless for the punishment of crime, shall ever be tolerated in this State.

§ 23. No person shall be imprisoned for debt, arising out of, or founded on a contract, express or implied; except in cases of fraud or breach of trust, or of moneys collected by public officers, or in any professional employment; and no person shall be imprisoned for a militia fine in time of peace.

§ 24. No person shall be rendered incompetent to be a witness on account of his opinions on matters of religious belief.

§ 25. Any citizen of this State who may hereafter be engaged, either directly or indirectly, in a duel, either as principal or accessory before the fact, shall forever be disqualified from holding any office under the constitution and laws of this State, nor be permitted to vote at any election.

§ 26. The assent of two-thirds of the members elected to each branch of the Legislature, shall be requisite to every bill appropriating the public moneys or property for local or private purposes.

§ 27. No lease or grant of agricultural land for a longer period than twelve years, hereafter made, in which shall be reserved any rent or service of any kind, shall be valid.

§ 28. No corporation shall hold any real estate hereafter acquired for a longer period than ten years, except such real estate as shall be actually occupied by such corporation in the exercise of its franchises.

§ 29. All lands, the title to which shall fail from a defect of heirs, shall escheat to the State, and shall be appropriated exclusively to the support of primary schools.

§ 30. All acts of the Legislature, contrary to this or any other article of this Constitution, shall be void.

ARTICLE —.

Elections.

§ 1. In all elections, every white male citizen above the age of twenty-one years, who shall have resided in this State three months next preceding any election; every white male inhabitant of the age aforesaid, who was permitted to vote under the provisions of the previous constitution of this State; and also every white male inhabitant of the age aforesaid, who shall have resided in the State two years and a half, and declared his intention to become a citizen of the United States; and every civilized male inhabitant of Indian descent, of the age aforesaid, not a member of any tribe, who shall be a native of the United States; and every white male inhabitant of the age aforesaid, who shall have been a resident of this State on the first day of January, A. D. 1850, shall be entitled to vote at such election; provided the last mentioned persons shall have declared their intention to become citizens of the United States, pursuant to the laws thereof, at least six months next preceding such election; but no such citizen or inhabitant shall be entitled to vote at any such election, unless he shall have resided in this State three months next preceding such election, nor in any township or ward, unless he is an actual resident thereof, and shall have resided therein for ten days next preceding such election.

§ 2. All votes shall be given by ballot, except for such township officers as may by law be directed to be otherwise chosen.

§ 3. Electors shall, in all cases except treason, felony, or breach of of the peace, be privileged from arrest during their attendance at election, and in going to and returning from the same.

§ 4. No elector shall be obliged to do militia duty on the day of election, except in time of war or public danger.

§ 5. For the purpose of voting, no person shall be deemed to have gained or lost a residence, by reason of his presence or absence while employed in the service of the United States or of this State; nor while engaged in the navigation of the waters of this State, or of the United States, or of the high seas; nor while a student of any seminary of learning; nor while kept at any alms-house or other asylum at public expense; nor while confined in any public prison.

§ 6. Laws may be passed to preserve the purity of elections, and guard against abuses of the elective franchise.

§ 7. No soldier, seaman, or marine, in the army or navy of the United States, shall be deemed a resident of this State, in consequence of being stationed in any military or naval place within the same.

RESOLUTION.

Resolved, That at the next general election, and at the same time when the votes of the electors shall be taken for the adoption or rejection of the revised Constitution, the additional amendment in the words following;

"Every colored male inhabitant, possessing the qualifications required by the first section of the second article of the Constitution, shall have the rights and privileges of an elector,"

Shall be separately submitted to the electors of this State for their adoption or rejection, in form following, to wit: A separate ballot may be given by every person having the right to vote for the revised Constitution, to be deposited in a separate box. Upon the ballot given for the adoption of the said separate amendment, shall be written or printed, or partly written and partly printed, the words "Equal suffrage to colored persons? Yes;" and upon all ballots given against the adoption of the said separate amendment, in like manner, the words, "Equal suffrage to colored persons? No." And on such ballots shall be written or printed, or partly written and partly printed, the words, "Constitution: Suffrage;" in such manner that such words shall appear on the outer side of such ballot when folded. If, at said election, a majority of all the votes given for and against the said separate amendment, shall contain the words "Equal suffrage to colored persons? Yes," then the said separate amendment shall be a separate section of article second of the Constitution, in full force and effect, any thing in the constitution to the contrary notwithstanding.

ARTICLE —.

Legislative Department.

§ 1. The legislative power shall be vested in a Senate and House of Representatives.

§ 2. The number of Representatives shall never be less than sixty-four, nor more than one hundred, and shall be chosen for two years, and by single districts; the Senate shall consist of thirty-two members, and the Senators, one from each district, shall be elected for two years.

§ 3. The Legislature shall provide by law for an enumeration of the inhabitants of this State in the year eighteen hundred and fifty-five, and at the end of every ten years thereafter; and at the first session after each enumeration so made, and also after each enumeration made by the authority of the United States, the Legislature shall apportion anew the Representatives and Senators among the several counties and districts, according to the number of white inhabitants and civilized persons of Indian descent, not members of any tribe; which apportionment shall remain unaltered until the return of another enumeration: *Provided,* That the county of Saginaw, with the territory thereto attached, shall be entitled to one Representative; the county of Tuscola, and the territory thereto attached, one Representative; the county of Sanilac, and the territory thereto attached, one Representative; the counties of Midland, Gratiot and Aronac, with the territory thereto attached, one Representative; the county of Montcalm, with the territory attached thereto, one Representative; and the counties of Newaygo and Oceana, with the territory attached thereto, one Representative; and each county hereafter organized, with such territory as may be attached thereto, shall be entitled to a separate Representative, when it shall have attained a population equal to a moiety of the ratio of representation.

§ 4. The boards of supervisors in such counties as may be entitled to more than one member of the House of Representatives, shall assemble at such time and place as the Legislature shall prescribe, and divide their respective counties into representative districts, equal to the number of Representatives to which such counties may severally be entitled by law, and shall cause to be filed in the offices of the Secretary of State and the clerks of their respective counties, a description of such representative districts, specifying the number of each district, and the population thereof, according to the last preceding enumeration, as near as can be ascertained. Each representative district shall contain, as nearly as may be, an equal number of white inhabitants, and shall consist of convenient and contiguous territory; but no township or city shall be divided in the formation of representative districts. And when any township or city shall contain a population which shall entitle it to more than one Representative, then such township or city shall elect the number of Representatives to which it shall be so entitled by general ticket.

§ 5. The State shall be divided into thirty-two districts, to be called Senate districts, each of which shall choose one Senator. The districts shall be numbered from one to thirty-two, inclusive. No county shall be divided in the formation of Senate districts, except such county shall be equitably entitled to two or more Senators.

§ 6. Senators and Representatives shall be citizens of the United States, and be qualified electors in the respective counties and districts which they represent; and a removal from their respective counties or districts shall be deemed a vacation of their seats.

§ 7. No persons holding any office under the United States or this State, or any county office, (notaries public, officers of the militia and officers elected by townships excepted,) shall be eligible to or have a seat in either house of the Legislature, and all votes given for any such person shall be void.

§ 8. Senators and Representatives shall, in all cases, except treason, felony or breach of the peace, be privilged from arrest; nor shall they be subject to any civil process during the session of the Legislature, nor for fifteen days next before the commencement and after the termination of each session; and for any speech in either house, they shall not be questioned in any other place.

§ 9. A majority of each house shall constitute a quorum to do business; but a smaller number may adjourn from day to day, and may compel the attendance of absent members, in such mannner and under such penalties as each house may provide.

§ 10. Each house shall choose its own officers, and shall determine the rules of its procedings, and judge of the qualifications, elections and returns of its own members; and may, with the concurrence of two-thirds of all the members elected, expel a member; but no member shall be expelled a second time for the same cause, nor for any cause known to his constituents antecedent to his election; and the reason for such expulsion shall be entered upon the journal, with the names of the members voting on the question.

§ 11. Each house shall keep a journal of its proceedings, and publish the same, except such parts as may require secrecy; and the yeas and nays of the members of either house, on any question, shall, at the request of one-fifth of the members elected, be entered on the journal. Any member of either house shall have liberty to dissent from and protest against any act, proceeding or resolution which he may think injurious to the public or an individual, and have the reason of his dissent entered on the journal.

§ 12. In all elections by either or both houses, the votes shall be given *viva voce;* and all votes on nominations made to the Senate, shall be taken by yeas and nays, and published with the journals of its proceedings.

§ 13. The doors of each house shall be open, except when the public welfare shall require secrecy. Neither house shall, without the consent of the other, adjourn for more than three days, nor to any other place than where the Legislature may then be in session.

§ 14. Any bill may originate in either house of the Legislature.

§ 15. Every bill passed by the Legislature shall, before it becomes a law, be presented to the Governor; if he approves it, he shall sign it; but if not, he shall return it with his objections to that house in which it originated, who shall enter the objections at large upon their journal, and proceed to reconsider it. If, after such reconsideration, two-thirds of all the members elected agree to pass the bill, it shall be sent, with the objections, to the other house, by whom it shall likewise be reconsidered; and if approved also by two-thirds of all the members elected to that house, it shall become a law; but in such case, the vote of both houses shall be determined by yeas and nays, and the names of the members voting for or against the bill shall be entered on the journals of each house respectively; and if any bill be not returned by the Governor within ten days, Sundays excepted, after it has been presented to him, the same shall become a law, in like manner as if he had signed it, unless the Legislature, by their adjournment, prevent its return; in which case it shall not become a law. But the Governor may approve and sign and file in the office of the Secretary of State, within five days after the adjournment of the two houses, any act passed during the last five days of the session; in which case it shall become a law.

§ 16. Every resolution, to which the concurrence of the Senate and House of Represenntatives may be necessary, except in case of adjournment, shall be presented to the Governor; and before the same shall take effect, shall be proceeded upon in the same manner as in the case of a bill.

§ 17. The members of the Legislature shall receive for their services only three dollars a day for actual attendance and when absent from sickness, for the first sixty days of the session of 1851, and for the first forty days of every subsequent session, and nothing thereafter. When convened in extra session by the Governor, they shall receive three dollars a day for the first twenty days, and nothing thereafter; and shall legislate on no other subjects than those expressly stated in the Governor's proclamation, or submitted to them by his special message. They shall also receive no more than ten cents for every mile they shall actually travel, in going to and returning from their place of meeting, on the usually traveled route; and for stationery and newspapers, not exceeding five dollars for each member during any session. Each member of the Legislature shall be entitled to one copy of the laws, journals and documents of the Legislature of which he was a member; but the Legislature shall not, at the expense of the State, provide for its members books, newspapers or other perquisites of office, not expressly authorized by this constitution.

§ 18. The Legislature may provide by law for the payment of postage on all mailable matter received by the members, Lieutenant Governor and Speaker, during the sessions of the Legislature, but not on any sent or mailed by them.

§ 19. The President of the Senate and the Speaker of the House of Representatives shall receive the same per diem compensation and mileage as members of the Legislature, and no more.

§ 20. No member of the Legislature shall receive any civil appointment within this State, or to the Senate of the United States, by the Governor, the Governor and Senate, from the Legislature, or any other State authority, during the term for which he shall have been elected; and all such appointments, and all votes given for any such member for any such office or appointment, shall be void; nor shall any member of the Legislature be interested, either directly or indirectly, in any contract with the State, or any county thereof, authorized by any law passed during the time for which he shall have been elected, and for one year thereafter.

§ 21. The Governor shall issue writs of election to fill such vacancancies as may occur in the Senate and House of Representatives.

§ 22. All bills and joint resolutions shall be read three times in each house before the final passage thereof; and no bill or joint resolution shall become a law without the concurrence of a majority of all the members elect in each house; and on the final passage of all bills, the vote shall be by yeas and nays, and shall be entered on the journal.

§ 23. No law shall embrace more than one object, which shall be expressed in its title; and no public act shall take effect or be in force until the expiration of ninety days from the end of the session at which the same may be passed, unless the Legislature, by a two-thirds vote of all the members elected to each house, shall otherwise direct.

§ 24. The Legislature shall never grant or authorize extra compensation to any public officer, agent, servant or contractor, after the service shall have been rendered or the contract entered into.

§ 25. The Legislature shall provide by law that the fuel and stationery furnished for the use of the State, the printing and binding the laws and journals, all blanks, paper and printing for the executive departments, and all other printing ordered by the Legislature, shall be let by contract to the lowest bidder or bidders, who shall give adequate and satisfactory security for the performance thereof. And it shall not be competent for the Legislature to rescind or alter such contract, or to release the person or persons taking the same, or his or their sureties, from the performance of any of the conditions of the contract; and no member of the Legislature, or other officer of the State, shall be interested, either directly or indirectly, in any such contract.

§ 26. The Legislature shall have no power to authorize, by private or special law, the sale or conveyance of any lands or other real estate belonging in whole or in part to any person or persons; nor to vacate or alter any road laid out by commissioners of highways, or any street in any incorporated city or village, or in any township plat.

§ 27. The Legislature may authorize the employment of a chaplain for the state prison, but no money shall be drawn from the treasury for the payment of any religious services in either branch of the Legislature.

§ 28. No law shall be revised or amended by reference to its title only; but the act revised, and the section or sections of the act amended, shall be re-enacted and published at length.

§ 29. Divorces shall not be granted by the Legislature; and no lottery shall be authorized, nor shall the sale of lottery tickets be permitted.

§ 30. No new bill shall be introduced into either house during the last three days of the session, unless by the unanimous consent of the house in which it originates.

§ 31. In case of contested elections, the person only shall receive from the State per diem compensation or mileage who is declared by the house in which the contest takes place, to be entitled to a seat.

§ 32. No person who may hereafter be a collector, or holder of public moneys, shall have a seat in either house of the Legislature, or be eligible to any office of trust or profit under this State, until he shall have accounted for and paid over, as provided by law, all sums for which he may be liable.

§ 33. The Legislature shall not audit or allow any private claim or account.

§ 34. Whenever the Legislature fixes upon the day of adjournment, they shall adjourn at twelve o'clock at noon of that day.

§ 35. The Legislature shall meet at the seat of government on the first Wednesday in February next, and on the first Wednesday of January of every second year thereafter, and at no other place or time, unless as provided by this Constitution.

§ 36. The election of Senators and Representatives, pursuant to the provisions of this Constitution, shall be held on the Tuesday succeeding the first Monday of November in the year 1852, and on the Tuesday succeeding the first Monday of November of every second year thereafter.

§ 37. The Legislature shall have no power to establish a State paper; but every newspaper in the State which shall publish all the general laws of any session within forty days of their passage, shall be entitled to receive a sum not exceeding fifteen dollars therefor.

§ 38. The style of the laws of this State shall be "The People of the State of Michigan enact."

§ 39. The Legislature shall have no power to pass any act to grant any license for the sale of ardent spirits or other intoxicating liquors.

ARTICLE —.

Executive Department.

§ 1. The Executive power shall be vested in a Governor, who shall hold his office for two years. A Lieutenant Governor shall be chosen at the same time and for the same term.

§ 2. No person shall be eligible to the office of Governor or Lieutenant Governor, who shall not have been five years a citizen of the United States, and a resident of this State two years next preceding his election; nor shall any person be eligible to the office of Governor who shall not have attained the age of thirty years.

§ 3. The Governor and Lieutenant Governor shall be elected at the times and places of choosing members of the Legislature; the persons respectively having the highest number of votes for Governor and Lieutenant Governor shall be elected; but in case two or more shall have an equal and the highest number of votes for Governor and Lieutenant Governor, the Legislature shall, by joint vote, choose one of the said persons so having an equal and the highest number of votes.

§ 4. The Governor shall be Commander-in-Chief of the military and naval forces of this State; and he shall have power to call forth the militia, to execute the laws of the State, to suppress insurrections, and to repel invasions.

§ 5. He shall transact all necessary business with the officers of government, civil and military; and may require information, in writing, from the officers of the Executive department, upon any subject relating to the duties of their respective offices.

§ 6. He shall take care that the laws be faithfully executed.

§ 7. He shall have power to convene the Legislature on extraordinary occasions. He shall communicate by message, at such times as he may deem necessary and proper, to the existing Legislature, and at the close of his official term of service, to the next Legislature, the condition of the State, and recommend such matters to them as he shall deem expedient.

§ 8. He may direct the Legislature to meet at some other place than the seat of government, if that shall become dangerous from a common enemy or disease.

§ 9. The Governor shall have the power to grant reprieves, commutations and pardons, after conviction, for all offences except treason and cases of impeachment, upon such conditions, and with such restrictions and limitations as he may think proper, subject to such regulations as may be provided by law, relative to the manner of applying for pardons. Upon conviction for treason, he shall have power to suspend the execution of the sentence until the case shall be reported to the Legislature at its next meeting, when the Legislature shall either pardon, or commute the sentence, direct the execution of the sentence, or grant a further reprieve. He shall communicate to the Legislature at each session, each case of reprieve, commutation or pardon granted; stating the name of the convict, the crime of which he was convicted, the sentence and its date, and the date of the reprieve, commutation or pardon.

§ 10. In case of the impeachment of the Governor, his removal from office, death, inability to discharge the powers and duties of the said office, resignation, or absence from the State, the powers and duties of the office shall devolve upon the Lieutenant Governor for the residue of the term, or until the disability shall cease. But when the Governor shall, with the consent of the Legislature, be out of the State in time of war, at the head of a military force thereof, he shall continue Commander-in-Chief of all the military force of the State.

§ 11. If, during a vacancy of the office of Governor, the Lieutenant Governor shall be impeached, displaced, resign, die, or be incapable of performing the duties of his office, or be absent from the State, the President of the Senate shall act as Governor until the vacancy be filled, or the disability shall cease.

§ 12. The Lieutenant Governor shall, by virtue of his office, be President of the Senate. In committee of the whole he may debate all questions; and when there is an equal division, he shall give the casting vote.

§ 13. No member of Congress, nor any other person holding office under the United States, or this State, shall execute the office of Governor; nor shall the Governor or Lieutenant Governor be eligible to any office or appointment from the Legislature, or either branch thereof, for the time for which they may have been elected; and all votes given for either of them for any such office shall be void.

§ 14. Whenever the office of Governor or Lieutenant Governor becomes vacated, the person executing the duties of Governor for the time being shall give notice thereof; and the electors shall, on the Tuesday succeeding the first Monday of November next, choose a person to fill such vacancy.

§ 15. The Lieutenant Governor and President of the Senate *pro tempore*, when performing the duties of Governor, shall receive the same compensation as is allowed to the Governor.

§ 16. The great seal of the State shall continue to be kept by the Secretary of State; and all official acts of the Governor, his approval of the laws excepted, shall thereby be authenticated.

ARTICLE —.

Of State Officers.

§ 1. There shall be a Secretary of State, a Superintendent of Public Instruction, a State Treasurer, a Commissioner of the Land Office, an Auditor General, elected at each biennial general election, who shall hold their respective offices for the term of two years, and each of whom shall keep an office at the seat of government, and shall perform such duties as may be prescribed by law.

§ 2. The terms of office of the incumbents to be elected under the foregoing provisions, shall commence on the first Wednesday of January, 1853, and of every second year thereafter.

§ 3. Whenever a vacancy shall occur in any of the above mentiontioned State offices, the Governor (by and with the advice and consent of the Senate, if in session,) shall fill the same by appointment, to continue until the office can be supplied by an election, at such time and in such manner as shall be provided for by law.

§ 4. The Secretary of State, State Treasurer and Commissioner of the State Land Office, shall constitute a Board of State Auditors, for the examination and adjustment of all claims against the State, not otherwise provided for by law, or specially referred by the Legislature to some other tribunal. And shall also constitute a Board of

State Canvassers, for determining the result of all elections for Governor, Lieutenant Governor, Judges and State officers, and of such other elections as shall by law be referred to said board.

§ 5. In all cases of two or more persons having an equal and the highest number of votes for any office, as canvassed by the Board of State Canvassers, the two houses of the Legislature, in joint convention, shall choose one of said persons to fill such office; and in all cases where the determination of the Board of State Canvassers shall be contested, the two houses, in joint convention, shall direct which person shall be deemed to have been duly elected.

ARTICLE —.

Impeachments and Removals from Office.

§ 1. The House of Representatives shall have the sole power of impeaching civil officers of the State, for corrupt conduct in office, or for crimes and misdemeanors; but a majority of all the members elected shall be necessary to direct an impeachment.

§ 2. All impeachments shall be tried by the Senate. When the Governor or Lieutenant Governor shall be tried, the Chief Justice of the Supreme Court shall preside. Before the trial of an impeachment, the members of the court shall take an oath or affirmation truly and impartially to try and determine the charge in question, according to the evidence; and no person shall be convicted without the concurrence of two-thirds of the members elect. Judgment, in case of impeachment, shall not extend further than removal from office; but the party convicted shall be liable to indictment and punishment according to law.

§ 3. The House of Representatives shall, when an impeachment is directed, elect from their own body three members, whose duty it shall be to prosecute impeachments. No impeachment shall be tried till the Legislature shall have adjourned *sine die;* when the Senate shall proceed to try such impeachment.

§ 4. No judicial officer shall exercise his office, after he shall have been impeached, until he shall be acquitted.

§ 5. The Governor may make a provisional appointment to fill the vacancy occasioned by the suspension of an officer until he shall have been acquitted, or until after the election and qualification of a successor.

§ 6. For any reasonable cause, which shall not be sufficient ground for the impeachment of the judges of any of the courts, the Governor shall remove any of them on a concurrent resolution of two-thirds of the members elected to each branch of the Legislature; but the cause or causes for which such removal may be required, shall be stated at length in the address.

§ 7. The Legislature shall provide by law for the removal of justices of the peace and other county, township and school district officers, in such manner and for such causes as to them shall seem just and proper.

ARTICLE —.

Finance and Taxation.

§ 1. 1st. All specific taxes, save those received from the mining companies of the Upper Peninsula, shall be applied in paying the interest upon the primary school, university and other educational funds, the principal and interest of the State debt, in the order herein recited, until the extinguishment of the State debt, other than the amounts due to the primary school, university and other educational funds, at which time said specific taxes shall be added to, and forever thereafter constitute a part of the proceeds of the primary school fund. The Legislature shall provide for an annual tax, sufficient, with other resources of the State, to pay the estimated expenses of the State, and the interest of the State debt. The Legislature shall also, by taxes, supply any deficiency which may occur in the resources of the State.

§ 2. 1st. The Legislature, in addition to the above named taxes, shall provide by law for a sinking fund of at least twenty thousand dollars a year, to commence in eighteen hundred and fifty-two, with compound interest at six per cent per annum, and an annual increase of at least five per cent. 2d. Said sinking fund shall be applied solely to the payment and extinguishment of the principal of the State debt, other than the amounts due to the University and the primary school funds;

and said tax shall be continued so long as shall be necessary to secure the extinguishment of the existing funded and fundable debt. 3d. Said fundable debt may only be funded or redeemed at a value not exceeding that established by law in eighteen hundred and forty-eight.

§ 3. The State may, to meet casual deficits or failures in revenues or expenses not provided for, contract debts; but such debts, direct and contingent, shall not in the aggregate, at any one time, exceed fifty thousand dollars; and the moneys arising from the loans creating such debts, shall be applied to the purposes for which they were obtained, or the payment of the debts so contracted, and for no other purpose whatever.

§ 4. The State may contract debts to repel invasion, suppress insurrection, and defend the State in time of war; but the money arising from the contracting of such debts shall be applied to the purpose for which it was raised, or to repay such debts, and to no other purpose whatever.

§ 5. No money shall be paid out of the treasury of this State, or any of its funds, or any of the funds under its management, except in pursuance of appropriations made by law.

§ 6. The credit of the State shall not in any manner be given or loaned to, or in aid of any individual, association or corporation.

§ 7. No scrip, certificate or other evidence of State indebtedness whatsoever, shall be issued, except for the redemption of stock previously issued, or for such debts as are expressly authorized in this article.

§ 8. The state shall never subscribe for, or become the owner of, or interested in the stock of any company, association or corporation.

§ 9. The State shall never be a party to, or interested in, any work of internal improvement, nor engaged in carrying out any such work, except in the expenditure of grants or donations of land or other property made to the State.

§ 10. The State may continue to collect all specific taxes now accruing to the treasury under existing laws. And the legislature may provide for the collection of specific taxes, from such banking, railroad, plank road, and other corporations, hereafter formed or created, as they may deem expedient.

§ 11. The Legislature shall provide a uniform rule of taxation, except upon property paying specific taxes; and taxes shall be levied upon such property as the Legislature shall prescribe.

§ 12. All assessments hereafter authorized shall be made upon property at its cash value.

§ 13. The Legislature shall provide by law for an equalization of assessments upon all taxable property, except that paying specific taxes, by a State Board, in eighteen hundred and fifty-one, and on every fifth year thereafter.

§ 14. Every law which imposes, continues or revives a tax, shall distinctly state the tax, and the object to which it is to be applied; and it shall not be sufficient to refer to any other law to fix such tax or object.

ARTICLE —.

Corporations.

§ 1. Corporations may be formed under general laws; but shall not be created by special act, except for municipal purposes. All laws passed pursuant to this section may be altered from time to time, or repealed.

§ 2. No banking law or law for banking purposes, or amendments thereof, shall have any force or effect until the same shall, after its passage, have been submitted to a vote of the electors of the State, at some general election, and been approved by a majority of the votes cast on that subject at such election.

§ 3. The officers and stockholders of every corporation or association for banking purposes, issuing bank notes or any kind of paper credits to circulate as money, shall be individually liable for all its debts which were contracted during the time of their being officers and stockholders of such corporation or association, and for one year thereafter.

§ 4. The Legislature shall provide by law for the registry of all bills or notes issued or put in circulation as money, and shall require security to the full amount of notes or bills so registered, in State stocks, which shall be deposited with the State Treasurer, bearing interest, or stocks of the United Stated States, for the redemption of such bills or notes in specie.

§ 5. In case of the insolvency of any bank or banking association, the holders of the notes or bills thereof issued or put in circulation as money, shall be entitled to preference in payment, over all other creditors of such bank or association.

§ 6. The Legislature shall have no power to pass any law authorizing or sanctioning in any manner, directly or indirectly, the suspension of specie payments by any person, association or corporation.

§ 7. The stockholders of all corporations and joint stock associations shall be individually responsible for all debts contracted for labor performed for such corporation or association.

§ 8. The Legislature shall pass no bill altering or amending any act of incorporation heretofore granted, without the assent of two-thirds of the members elect to each house; nor shall any act of incorporation, heretofore granted, be renewed or extended. The provisions of this section shall not apply to municipal corporations.

§ 9. The State shall not become subscriber to the stock of any corporation or joint stock association.

§ 10. The property of no individual shall be taken by any corporation for public use, without compensation being first made or secured, in such manner as may be prescribed by law.

§ 11. No corporation hereafter to be created, except for the construction of rail roads and canals, shall ever endure for a longer term than thirty years, except those which are municipal.

§ 12. The term "corporations," as used in this article, shall be construed to include all associations and joint stock companies having any of the powers or privileges of corporations, not possessed by individuals or partnerships. And all corporations shall have the right to sue, and shall be subject to be sued, in all courts, in like cases as natural persons.

ARTICLE —.

County Officers and County Government.

§ 1. Each county, duly organized by law, shall be a body corporate and politic, with such rights, duties, powers, privileges and immunities as shall be established by law. All suits and proceedings, by or against any county, shall be in the name thereof.

§ 2. No county, now organized by law, shall ever be reduced by the organization of new counties to less than sixteen townships, as surveyed by the United States, unless a majority of the qualified electors residing in each county to be affected by such organization shall so elect. But the Legislature shall have power to organize any city into a separate county, when it shall have attained a population of at least twenty thousand people, without reference to geographical extent, when a majority of the legal voters of a county in which such city may be situated shall recommend such new organization.

§ 3. In each organized county there shall be one sheriff, a county clerk, a county treasurer, a register of deeds, one county surveyor, a prosecuting attorney, chosen by the qualified electors thereof, once in two years, and as often as vacancies shall happen, and whose duties and powers shall be prescribed by law. It shall be competent for the board of supervisors in the several counties to combine the offices of county clerk and register of deeds in one office, or discontinue the same.

§ 3. The county clerk, county treasurer, judge of probate and register of deeds, shall hold their offices at the county seat.

§ 5. The sheriff shall hold no other office, and shall be incapable of holding the office of sheriff longer than four in any term of six years. He may be required by law to renew his security from time to time, and in default of giving such security, his office shall be deemed vacant; but the county shall never be made responsible for his acts.

§ 6. A board of supervisors, consisting of one to be chosen from each organized township, shall be established in each county, with such powers and compensation as are prescribed in this constitution, and as shall be prescribed by law.

§ 7. All incorporated cities shall have such representation in the board of supervisors of the counties in which they are situated, as the Legislature may direct.

§ 8. No county seat, when once established, shall be removed, until the place to which it is proposed to be removed shall be designated by two-thirds of the board of supervisors of said county, and a majority of the qualified electors voting thereon shall have voted in favor of the proposed location, in such manner as shall be prescribed by law.

§ 9. The board of supervisors of any county may borrow or raise by tax one thousand dollars, for constructing or repairing public buildings, highways or bridges; but no greater sum shall be borrowed or raised by tax for such purpose in any one year, unless authorized by the votes of a majority of the electors of said county voting on that subject.

§ 10. The board of supervisors, or in the county of Wayne the board of county auditors, shall have the exclusive power to prescribe and fix the compensation for all services rendered for, and to adjust all claims against their respective counties, and the sum so fixed or defined shall be subject to no appeal.

§ 11. The boards of supervisors of all organized counties shall have the power to provide for the laying out of highways and the construction of bridges, and for the organizing of townships, under such restrictions and limitations as shall be prescribed by law; and the Legislature may hereafter confer upon the board of supervisors of the several counties of this State, such further powers of local legislation and administration as they may deem proper.

ARTICLE —.

Mode of Amending and Revising the Constitution.

§ 1. Any amendment or amendments to this constitution may be proposed in the Senate or House of Representatives; and if the same shall be agreed to by two-thirds of the members elected to the two houses, such proposed amendment or amendments shall be entered on their journals respectively, with the yeas and nays taken thereon; and shall be submitted to the people at such time and in such manner as the Legislature may provide. And if the people shall ratify and approve such amendment or amendments by a majority of the electors qualified to vote for members of the Legislature voting thereon, such amendment or amendments shall become part of this constitution.

§ 2. At the general election to be held in the year eighteen hundred and sixty-six, and in each sixteenth year thereafter, and also at such times as the Legislature may by law provide, the question of a general revision of the constitution shall be submitted to the electors qualified to vote for members of the Legislature; and in case a majority of the electors so qualified, voting at such election, shall decide in favor of a convention for such purpose, the legislature, at its next session, shall provide by law for the election of delegates to such convention.

ARTICLE —.

Division of the Powers of Government.

§ 1. The powers of this government shall be divided into three distinct departments—the Legislative, Executive and Judicial.

§ 2. No person or persons belonging to any of these departments, nor either of the departments, shall exercise any of the powers properly belonging to either of the others, except in the cases expressly provided for in this constitution.

ARTICLE —.

Militia.

§ 1. The militia of this State shall be composed of all able bodied white male citizens between the ages of eighteen and forty-five years, except such as are, or may hereafter be exempt by laws of the United States or of this State. But all such inhabitants of this State, of any religious denomination whatever, as, from scruples of conscience, may be averse to bearing arms, shall be excused therefrom, upon such conditions as shall be prescribed by law.

§ 2. The Legislature shall provide by law for organizing, equipping and disciplining the militia, in such manner as they shall deem expedient, not incompatible with the laws of the United States.

§ 3. Officers of the militia shall be elected or appointed in such manner as the Legislature shall from time to time direct, and shall be commissioned in such manner as may be provided by law.

ARTICLE —.

Exemptions and the Rights of Married Women.

§ 1. The personal property of every resident of this State, to consist of such articles as shall be designated by law, shall be exempted to the amount of not less than five hundred dollars from sale on execution or other final process of any court of law or equity, issued for the collection of any debt contracted after the adoption of this constitution.

§ 2. The homested of every family, of not less than forty acres, which shall not be included in any city, village or recorded town plat; or in lieu thereof, any lot in any city, village, or recorded town plat, or such parts of lots as shall be equal thereto, not exceeding in value fifteen hundred dollars, shall not be subject to forced sale for any debt hereafter incurred; nor shall the owner of such homestead, if a married man, alienate the same by any deed of conveyance, without the consent of his wife, obtained in due form of law.

§ 3. The homested of any family, after the death of the owner thereof, shall likewise be exempt from the payment of his debts, contracted after the adoption of this constitution, in all cases where any minor children shall survive the death of such owner.

§ 4. Whenever the owner of any homested shall decease, leaving a widow, but no children, the same shall also be exempt, and the rents and profits thereof shall accrue to her benefit during the time she shall remain a widow; provided she be not the owner of a homested in her own right.

§ 5. The real and personal estate of every female, acquired before marriage, and all property to which she may afterwards become entitled, by any gift, grant, inheritence or devise, shall be and remain the estate and property of such female, and shall not be liable for the debts, obligations or engagements of her husband; and she may devise the same as if she were unmarried.

ARTICLE —.

Of Cities and Villages.

§ 1. It shall be the duty of the Legislature to provide for the organization of cities and incorporated villages, and to restrict their powers of taxation, assessment, borrowing money, contracting debts, and loaning their credit, so as to prevent abuses in assessments and in contracting debts by such corporations.

§ 2. All judicial officers of cities and villages shall be elected at such time and in such manner as the Legislature may direct; all other officers of such cities and villages shall be elected by the electors thereof, or appointed by such authorities thereof as the Legislature shall designate for that purpose.

§ 3. Private property shall not be taken for improvements in cities and villages without the consent of the owner, unless the compensation therefor shall first be determined by a jury of freeholders, and actually paid or tendered in the manner to be provided by law.

§ 4. Previous notice of any application for an alteration of the charter of any corporation, shall be given in such manner as the Legislature shall by law direct.

ARTICLE —

Seat of Government.

§ 1. The seat of government of the State shall be in the township of Lansing in the county of Ingham, where it is now located.

ARTICLE —

Township Officers and Government.

§ 1. There shall be elected by the people annually, on the first Monday of April, in each organized township, one supervisor, one township clerk, who shall be *ex-officio* school inspector, one township treasurer, one school inspector, not exceeding four constables, and one overseer of highways for each highway district in such township, in whom, together with the justices of the peace, not to exceed four, shall be vested the township government, to be defined and limited in such manner as the Legislature shall prescribe.

§ 2. Each township, duly organized by law, shall be a body corporate and politic, with such rights, duties, powers, privileges and immunities, and such powers of local legislation, to be uniform throughout the State, as shall be prescribed by law. All suits and proceedings by or against any township, shall be in the name thereof.

ARTICLE —.

Education.

§ 1. The Superintendent of Public Instruction shall have the general supervision of public instruction, and his duties shall be prescribed by law.

§ 2. The proceeds from the sale of all lands that have been or hereafter may be granted by the United States to this State, for the support of schools, shall be and remain a perpetual fund, the interest of which, together with the rents of all such lands as remain unsold, shall be inviolably appropriated to the support of primary schools throughout the State, and shall be annually distributed for such purpose, upon such fair and equitable basis as shall be provided by law.

§ 3. The Legislature shall, within five years from the adoption of this constitution, provide for and establish a system of common schools. Such schools shall be kept without charge for tuition, for at least three months in each year, in every school district in the State, and all instruction in said schools shall be conducted in the English language.

§ 4. Any school district neglecting to keep up and support a school for three months in each year, shall be deprived of its proportion of the income of the primary school fund, and of all funds arising from tax for the support of schools.

§ 5. There shall be elected in each judicial circuit, at the time of the election of the judge of said circuit, a regent of the University, whose term of office shall be the same as that of said judges; and the regents thus elected shall constitute the Board of Regents of the University of Michigan.

§ 6. The regents elected pursuant to the provisions of the foregoing section, and their successors in office, shall continue to constitute the body corporate, known by the name and style of "the Regents of the University of Michigan."

§ 7. The regents of the University shall, at their first annual meeting, or as soon thereafter as may be, elect a President of the University of Michigan, who shall be *ex officio* a member of their board, and shall preside at the meetings of said regents, and who shall be the principal executive officer, with the privilege of speaking but not of voting, of the University. Said board of regents shall have the general supervision of the University, and the direction and control of all expenditures from the University interest fund.

§ 8. The proceeds from the sale of all lands that have been or may hereafter be granted by the United States to this State, for the support of a University, and all funds accruing from any other source, for the purpose aforesaid, shall be and remain a perpetual fund, the interest of which, together with the rents of all such lands as may remain unsold, shall be inviolably appropriated to the support of the University, with such branches as the public good may require, for the promotion of literature and the arts and sciences.

§ 9. There shall be elected at the first general election in this State, after the ratification of this constitution, three members of the State Board of Education, one for the term of two years, one for the term of four years, and one for the term of six years; and at each succeeding biennial election, there shall be one member of said board elected, who shall hold his office for the term of six years. The Superintendent of Public Instruction shall be *ex officio* a member and secretary of said board. Said board shall have the general supervision of the State Normal School, and their duties shall be prescribed by law.

§ 10. The proceeds from the sale of all lands that have been or shall be hereafter granted or appropriated for the use of the State Normal School, shall be and remain a perpetual fund, the interest of which, together with the rents and profits of such of said lands as shall remain unsold, shall be inviolably appropriated for the support of said Normal School, according to the terms of the grant or appropriation.

§ 11. Institutions for the benefit of those inhabitants who are deaf, dumb, blind or insane, shall always be fostered and supported, and the proceeds from the sale of all lands that have been or shall be hereafter granted or appropriated for the support of such institutions, shall be inviolably appropriated according to the terms and conditions of such grant or appropriation.

§ 12. The Legislature shall encourage, by all suitable means, the promotion of intellectual, scientific and agricultural improvement; and shall, as soon as practicable, provide for the establishment of an agricultural school. And it shall be competent for the legislature to appropriate the twenty-two sections of salt spring lands now unappropriated, or the money arising from the sale of the same, where such lands have been already sold, and any land which may hereafter be granted or appropriated for such purpose, for the support and maintenance of such school, and it shall be competent for the legislature to make the same a branch of the University for instruction in agriculture and the natural sciences connected therewith, and place the same under the supervision of the Regents of the University. And the proceeds of the sale of all such lands that have been, or that may be hereafter sold, shall be a perpetual fund, the interest of which, together with the rents and profits of such lands, shall be appropriated for the support of such school until otherwise appropriated by law. The Legislature shall also provide for the establishment of at least one library in each township; and all fines assessesed and collected in the several counties for any breach of the penal laws, shall be exclusively applied to the support of said libraries.

ARTICLE —

Judicial Department.

§ 1. The judicial power is vested in one supreme court, in circuit courts, in probate courts, and in justices of the peace. Municipal courts of civil and criminal jurisdiction may be established by the Legislature in cities.

§ 2. For the term of six years, and thereafter, until the Legislature shall otherwise provide, the judges of the several circuit courts shall be judges of the supreme court, four of whom shall constitute a quorum, and a concurrence of three shall be necessary to a final decision. The Legislature shall have power, if they should think expedient and necessary, after six years, to provide by law for the organization of a separate supreme court, with the jurisdiction and powers prescribed in this constitution, to consist of one chief justice and three associate justices, to be elected by the qualified electors of the State. The separate court, when so organized, shall not be changed or discontinued by the Legislature for eight years after its organization. The judges thereof, shall be so classified that but one of them shall go out of office at the same time, and their term of office shall be eight years.

§ 3. The supreme court shall have a general superintending control over all inferior courts, and shall have power to issue writs of error, habeas corpus, mandamus, injunction, quo warranto, certiorari, and other original and remedial writs, and to hear and determine the same. In all other cases it shall have appellate jurisdiction only.

§ 4. Four terms of the supreme court shall be he held annually, at such times and places as may be designated by law.

§ 5. It shall be the duty of the supreme court, by general rules, to establish, modify and amend the practice in said court and in the circuit courts, and simplify the same so far as practicable; and testimony in cases in equity shall be taken in like manner as in cases at law, and the office of master in chancery is hereby prohibited. And the Legislature shall, as far as practicable, abolish all distinction between law and equity proceedings.

§ 6. The State shall be divided into eight judicial circuits; in each of which one circuit judge shall be elected by the qualified electors thereof, and who shall hold his office for the term of six years, and until his successor is elected and qualified.

§ 7. The Legislature may alter the limits of circuits or increase the number of the same. No alteration or increase shall have the effect to remove a judge from office. In every additional circuit established the judge shall be elected by the qualified electors of said circuit, and his term of office shall continue as provided in this constitution for judges of the circuit court.

§ 8. The circuit courts shall have original jurisdiction in all matters civil and criminal, not excepted in this constitution, and not prohibited by law; and appellate jurisdiction from all inferior courts and tribunals, and a supervisory control of the same. They shall also have power to issue writs of habeas corpus, mandamus, injunction, quo warranto, certiorari and other writs necessary to carry into effect their orders, judgments and decrees, and give them a general control over inferior courts and tribunals within their respective jurisdictions.

§ 9. Each of the judges of the circuit courts shall receive a salary payable quarterly. They shall receive no fees or perquisites of office, or other compensation; and shall be ineligible to any other than a judicial office during the term for which they are elected, and for one year thereafter. All votes for either of them, for any office other than the one held by them, given either by the Legislature or the people, shall be void.

§ 10. The supreme court may appoint a reporter of its decisions. The decisions made by the supreme court shall be in writing, and signed by the judges concurring therein; and any judge dissenting therefrom, shall give the reasons of such dissent in writing, under his signature; and all said opinions shall be filed in the office of the clerk of said supreme court. The judges of the circuit courts within their respective jurisdictions, may fill vacancies in the office of county clerk and of prosecuting attorney; but no judge of the supreme court, or of a circuit court, shall exercise any other power of appointment to public office.

§ 11. A circuit court shall be held at least twice in each year in every county organized for judicial purposes, and in counties containing ten thousand inhabitants, a circuit court shall be held four times a year. Judges of the circuit court may hold courts for each other, and shall do so when required by law.

§ 12. The clerk of each county organized for judicial purposes shall be the clerk of the circuit court of such county, and of the supreme court when held within the same.

§ 13. In each of the counties organized for judicial purposes, there shall be a court of probate. The judge of such court shall be elected by the qualified electors of the county in which he resides, and shall hold his office for four years, and until his successor is elected and qualified. The jurisdiction, powers and duties of such court shall be prescribed by law.

§ 14. When a vacancy occurs in the office of judge of the supreme court, circuit court or probate court, such vacancy shall be filled by appointment of the governor, which shall continue until a successor is elected and qualified; and when elected, such successor shall hold his office the residue of the unexpired term.

§ 15. The supreme court, the circuit and probate courts of each county, shall be courts of record, and shall each have a common seal.

§ 16. The Legislature may provide by law for the election of one or more persons in each organized county, who may be vested with judicial powers, not exceeding those of a judge of the circuit court at chambers. In counties having a population of less than ten thousand inhabitants, by the last preceding enumeration provided for in this constitution, these powers may be devolved upon the judge of probate.

§ 17. There shall be not exceeding four justices of the peace in each organized township. They shall be elected by the qualified electors of the township, and shall hold their offices for four years, and until their successors are elected and qualified. They shall have civil jurisdiction to the amount of three hundred dollars, and concurrent jurisdiction to the amount of five hundred dollars, and such criminal jurisdiction and perform such duties as may be prescribed by law. At the first election in any township, they shall be classified by law in such manner that one justice shall be elected annually in each township thereafter. The Legislature may increase the number of justices in cities.

§ 18. Judges of the supreme court, circuit judges, and justices of the peace, shall be conservators of the peace within their respectives jurisdictions.

§ 19. The first election of judges of the circuit courts, shall be held on the first Monday in April, 1851; and for the election of judges of the probate courts on the Tuesday succeeding the 1st Monday of November 1852, and every sixth year thereafter an election shall be held for judges of the circuit court, and every fourth year thereafter for judges of probate. Whenever an additional circuit is created, such provision may be made as to hold the subsequent election of such additional judge at the regular elections herein provided.

§ 20. Whenever a judge shall remove beyond the limits of the circuit for which he was elected, and whenever a justice of the peace shall remove from the township in which he was elected, or who, by a change in the boundaries of said township, shall be placed without the same, shall be deemed to have vacated their respective offices.

§ 21. The Legislature shall have power to establish courts of conciliation, with powers and duties prescribed by law.

§ 22. The style of all process shall be: "In the name of the people of the State of Michigan." All indictments shall conclude: "against the peace of the people of the State of Michigan."

§ 23. Every person of the age of 21 years, of good moral character, shall have the right to practice in any court in this State.

www.ingramcontent.com/pod-product-compliance
Lightning Source LLC
LaVergne TN
LVHW010743120826
845150LV00009B/2282
* 9 7 8 1 4 1 8 1 9 4 4 2 0 *